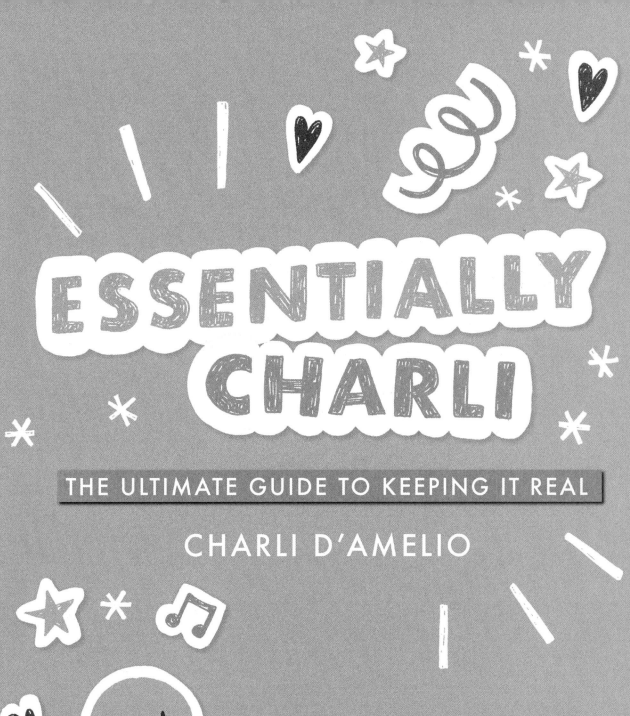

ESSENTIALLY CHARLI

THE ULTIMATE GUIDE TO KEEPING IT REAL

CHARLI D'AMELIO

CHARLI D'AMELIO

ESSENTIALLY CHARLI!

Amulet Books * New York

Library of Congress Control Number 2020943636

ISBN 978-1-4197-5232-2

Text copyright © 2020 Charli D'Amelio
Illustrations copyright © 2020 Steph Stilwell
Book design by Steph Stilwell

Printed and bound in U.S.A.
10 9 8 7 6 5 4 3 2

Amulet Books are available at special discounts when purchased in quantity
for premiums and promotions as well as fundraising or educational use.
Special editions can also be created to specification. For details, contact
specialsales@abramsbooks.com or the address below.

ABRAMS The Art of Books
195 Broadway, New York, NY 10007
abramsbooks.com

FOR THE PEOPLE
WHO SUPPORT ME

CONTENTS

PART ONE

CHILDHOOD

Flip corner to see Charli DANCE!

I was born and raised in Connecticut. I started dancing at a very young age. I was crazy when I was little—my whole life revolved around dance! I'm talking forty-eight hours per week from the time I was five. I was three years old performing onstage. During my first-ever "performance" on stage, I didn't move after my sunglasses got stuck to my snowman costume!

What's your first embarrassing
or hilarious memory?

SWEET SIXTEEN!

I practically lived at the dance studio as a kid, but I did it because it was fun. I only recently set up my first private studio at home! I didn't have much of a social life early on, because if anyone asked me to do anything other than dance, I'd be like . . . no thanks! (What do people even wear when they go out to dinner? I still don't know. Leggings?)

MY BEST FRIEND FROM CHILDHOOD IS ALSO A DANCER, AND DANCE IS REALLY IMPORTANT TO OUR FRIENDSHIP.

DANCE DANCE DANCE

REAL TALK

I can imagine dancing for the rest of my life. Hopefully as a career, but definitely just for fun.

When I was a kid, I had a stuffed penguin that I still keep around. It doesn't have a name. Then my grandfather gave me a second stuffed penguin. My grandfather passed when I was nine years old, and I put one of the penguins in his casket. So now, whenever people ask me what my favorite animal is, I say a penguin. It's a little sentimental thing I have, and it's a nice memory of my grandfather.

I am so lucky to have my big sister, Dixie, in my life. We've been through so much together and I really can't imagine being the person I am today without her.

What's a sentimental object you own, and what's the story behind it?

When I was a kid, I liked to read mysteries and true crime books.

My grandfather was an amazing carpenter who did architecture and built the house that my grandma lives in now. He'd take me into his shop and do wood art with me. He also had a boat—it was never in the water; it was always sitting in the driveway at his house. We'd sit in that boat forever, me and my cousins.

We got Rebel, my chocolate Lab, just after my grandfather passed away. We named her Rebel because it felt like a sign.

Rebel and I have always had some type of special connection. I like big dogs, and she's really fun to be around. My family has three other dogs: Cali, a golden retriever; Cody, a cockapoo; and Belle, a Havanese.

PUPPY LOVE

CHARLI TRIVIA

My favorite Halloween costumes so far have been Judge Judy, a candy corn, and the girl from *The Ring*. I love horror movies, and I loved being a scary creature.

PART TWO

FRIENDSHIP

TRUE FRIENDS ARE THE ONES WHO MAKE YOU FEEL LIKE YOU CAN BE COMPLETELY YOURSELF.

Some of my best friends knew me before I was in the public eye, and I'm just as close to them today as we were before. I've been lucky to make a ton of new friends lately. It's been so great to bring my old friends and new friends together. My newer friends from L.A. will comment on some of my Connecticut friends' posts, and it's really nice to see, because they don't know each other yet beyond having me in their lives. It makes me really happy when they comment on each other's content on social media—even though they don't actually know each other, they're still supportive, kind, and excited to one day meet IRL.

REAL TALK
I hope people who read this book get to know me a little—who I really am, not just that girl on TikTok.

MY FRIENDS ARE ALL VERY DIFFERENT TYPES OF PEOPLE, BUT I LOVE THEM FOR HOW THEY MAKE ME FEEL.

BESTIES

TO MY FELLOW SHY PEOPLE: DON'T LET WHAT OTHER PEOPLE SAY HAVE ANY EFFECT ON YOU.

Just about to go onstage with Bebe Rexha! I was so nervous but the second I got on stage, I lost myself in the performance and regained confidence!

BARCLAYS CENTER

B1-B15   VIP ENTRY   LOGES LG1-LG5   SECTION 31-1...

BE CONFIDENT IN WHO YOU ARE

YOU GOT THIS!

One of the most positive results of putting myself out there on social media has been a newfound sense of confidence. For me, confidence first manifested in the clothes I wear. That's one of the biggest ways I've evolved, because previously I believed that I couldn't wear whatever I wanted. Now I can just relax and be confident in myself. I wear whatever I want and feel fine with it. Now that I'm more confident, it's easier to meet people and make friends. Not everyone's gonna like you, and that's fine! You need to get past that and work more on yourself. Sometimes it takes a while, but it'll all click into place eventually.

ROLE MODELS!

Lady Gaga and J.Lo. are two of my role models. I was lucky enough to meet J.Lo already and hope to meet Lady Gaga one day.

I look up to so many people, but my friends most of all. Without naming names ☺, here's why:

* She's very outgoing and has a strong personality.
* She has the vibe of "You can say whatever you want about me and nothing's going to hurt me, because I'm not going to stoop to your level!"
* She's super hardworking, even when it's tough.
* He's helped me through many hard times.
* No matter what she's going through, she always has her priorities on track!
* Whatever she's doing, she makes sure she loves it.
* He gives 100% to everything he does. (That's really difficult in the social media world, because social media is very taxing and time-consuming—it involves a lot of preparation of posts and giving of yourself to fans. Even though it's fun, sometimes it feels like you're always "on"!)

HARDWORKING

SUPPORTIVE

PASSIONATE

What qualities do you love in your friends?

CHARLI TRIVIA

My ideal night out with friends would be just driving around—going to get ice cream and listening to music.

FUN TIMES

If I could guest star on any TV show, it would be *American Horror Story*. It's so fun. "Coven" was my favorite season.

TRAVELING WITH YOUR BEST FRIENDS IS SO MUCH FUN.

FUN IN THE SUN

My friend group LOVES traveling with each other. The best trip I've ever taken was to Hawaii with all my friends. That was so much fun! We had a villa all to ourselves—it was amazing to be living with my best friends for a week. But my favorite place in the world is the Bahamas. I used to go there when I was little. And I got to go there with all my friends recently and relive my childhood memories! It's fun when you're older and can walk around at night and it's warm . . . Hawaii was more for the experiences. The Bahamas, I love for the landscape.

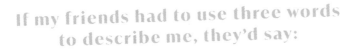

If my friends had to use three words to describe me, they'd say:

ENERGETIC, ENTERTAINING (I'M FUN TO WATCH WHEN I DANCE IN PUBLIC), AND GENUINE.

What three words would your friends use to describe you?

ONE THING I'VE LEARNED IS THAT IT'S REALLY IMPORTANT TO LOOK BEYOND LABELS WHEN YOU'RE CHOOSING YOUR FRIENDS.

HANGIN' OUT

REAL TALK

Nervous about meeting a new friend? A great way to break the ice and get to know someone better is to be curious and ask them questions about their life.

BE YOU

A lot of my friends now aren't the same people I was friends with in middle school. There was all kinds of eighth-grade drama that now we look back and laugh at. A lot of people are given labels or put into boxes that have nothing to do with them. I'm so glad I started being smarter about getting to know people for who they really are. Now I'm friends with people based on how they make me feel—if I can be fully myself around them. I love my friends!

Do you have any friendships
that have surprised you?

_____

_____

_____

_____

_____

_____

_____

_____

FRIENDSHIP

PART THREE

FASHION

I grew up always wearing my dance clothes. Right now, when I'm not wearing leggings and a sweatshirt, I'm most comfortable in high-waisted jeans and crop tops—and I love all kinds of jackets!

I would describe my style as comfy chic— whatever I feel like wearing!

COMFY CHIC

How would you describe your style?

WHEN I WAS INVITED BY PRADA TO MILAN FASHION WEEK, I WAS A LITTLE NERVOUS, BUT I FELT SO LUCKY TO BE AROUND PEOPLE WHO KNEW HIGH FASHION, BECAUSE IT WAS NEW TO ME.

MILAN WAS SO COOL!

I couldn't believe it when I first received the invitation. Everyone around me knew fashion, but I'm just the girl who wears sweatshirts and leggings and dances for fun! I had never even been to a fashion show before. Everything about that trip was so glam—I even spotted Bella and Gigi Hadid in a hotel restaurant. It was crazy!

Prada, who dressed me for the event, really got my style. They picked stuff for me that felt like what I'd normally wear, only at a high-fashion level. I loved everything about that experience.

GLAM

I don't really shop. I just wear all my big sister's clothes! I hate going shopping, but Dixie is good at it. I don't have energy to try on clothes and all that stuff. But I *really* like purses. My favorite purse is astrology themed.

What's your favorite thing in your closet right now?

PART FOUR

GROWING UP

I'VE CHANGED IN A FEW BIG WAYS AS I'VE GROWN OLDER:

* I've gained a lot more confidence!
* I've been able to do so many amazing things.
* I've never been a super open person, but now I'm able to be less nervous around new people.
* No matter who I'm with, I can make friends, and I can make anyone feel welcome.
* I now know I'm a little offbeat, but it's not a bad thing.
* I am fully realizing who I always was but never got a chance to explore.

CONFIDENCE

OPPORTUNITIES

FRIENDLINESS

Even though I've been able to grow on social media, inside I'm still the same person I always was. What's different is that I have a lot more opportunities that I'm grateful for. I'm having so much fun trying new things!

UNIQUENESS

SENSE OF SELF

I'VE LEARNED THAT LIFE OFTEN DOESN'T WORK OUT THE WAY YOU PLAN— SOMETIMES IT'S EVEN BETTER.

BE FLEXIBLE AND OPEN TO CHANGE

EVERYTHING WORKS OUT

REAL TALK

Every now and then I hope things will work out a certain way, and they don't. But that's not a bad thing! Even though you can't always control the exact outcome, in the end everything tends to work out the way it should.

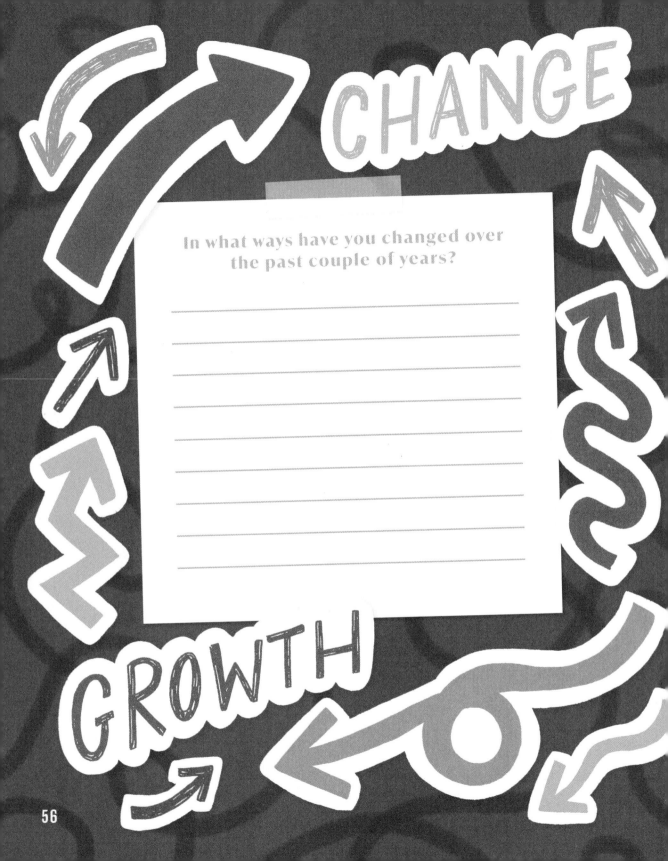

In what ways have you changed over the past couple of years?

CHANGE

GROWTH

I'VE ALWAYS BELIEVED IN ORDER TO FIGURE OUT WHAT YOU LIKE AND WHO YOU WANT TO BE, YOU HAVE TO TRY EVERYTHING ONCE.

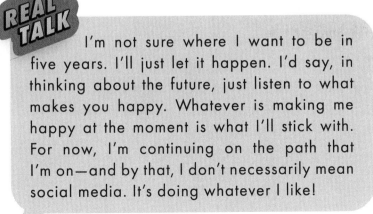

REAL TALK

I'm not sure where I want to be in five years. I'll just let it happen. I'd say, in thinking about the future, just listen to what makes you happy. Whatever is making me happy at the moment is what I'll stick with. For now, I'm continuing on the path that I'm on—and by that, I don't necessarily mean social media. It's doing whatever I like!

As you grow up, you're still learning and figuring out who you are. Don't feel like you have to do the same things as everyone else—but it's also OK to fit in, if that feels right to you. Trust yourself.

IT'S OK TO BE DIFFERENT

REAL TALK I go to school online now, but in the past, my teachers described me as diligent, respectful, and hardworking. All my teachers really liked me. I always made good grades and was engaged in class, got my work done, and listened carefully.

BE TRUE TO YOURSELF

Personally, I liked getting to know people from all different groups in school.

You can learn a lot from people who have different experiences or viewpoints than you do. Be open-minded, don't make assumptions about people, and ask them questions about themselves. It's a great way to break the ice and get to know someone better. You might even make a new friend!

LABELS DON'T MATTER

I WOULD LOVE TO GO TO COLLEGE. I PROBABLY WILL. IT DEPENDS ON WHAT I'M DOING AND WHATEVER IS GOING ON AT THE TIME. NO MATTER WHAT, I CAN ALWAYS GO TO COLLEGE AT SOME POINT IF I WANT TO.

Have you thought about whether you want to go to college, or where?

_____

_____

_____

_____

_____

_____

_____

What makes you want to go to college or to seek another path?

_____

_____

_____

_____

_____

_____

_____

OF EVERYONE
IN THE WORLD,
I ALWAYS HOLD
MYSELF MOST
ACCOUNTABLE.

The only time my social media following gets overwhelming is when I want to share how I'm feeling, but I don't want others to see me feeling down. That's one of the hardest parts. But I'm working on myself and making sure everything I say is what I mean, if that makes sense!

I DON'T OFTEN TALK ABOUT STUFF I'VE GONE THROUGH. BUT I'VE DEFINITELY BEEN IN TOUGH PLACES. I'VE HAD TO GO TO THERAPY AND GET HELP AND MAKE SURE I'M MENTALLY OK.

MENTAL HEALTH MATTERS

REAL TALK

When I'm in a bad mood, I just don't talk, or I dance. It depends on how I'm feeling.

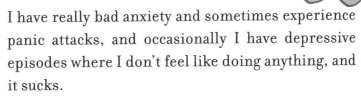

I have really bad anxiety and sometimes experience panic attacks, and occasionally I have depressive episodes where I don't feel like doing anything, and it sucks.

BUT THAT'S REAL LIFE.

It's hard to talk about, but it's also so important to open up. That can be tough for me, because when I try to talk about the stress that's related to newfound attention, some people say, "You've asked for this." Life can be tough no matter who you are and what you're dealing with! I let myself feel both the good and the bad and do the best I can.

Was there a time that you felt sad or anxious, and how did you deal with it?

_____

_____

_____

_____

_____

_____

_____

_____

BE KIND TO YOURSELF

IF I HAD A SUPERPOWER, IT WOULD BE TO GO BACK IN TIME.

REAL TALK

I'd go back and fix the little embarrassing things I did. I would not have gotten clear braces! I would not have gotten glasses as thick as I did. I wouldn't have worn the same four outfits every day. I would time travel in my own life but also to different eras, but only for a little bit. (I like the time I live in.) But I want clothes from the '80s to come back! I watched *Can't Buy Me Love* the other day and was like OH, THE OUTFITS.

FLASHBACK

I got my room redone for my birthday!

I have a lot of throw pillows on my bed—my favorite is embroidered with *I lied about being the outdoors type.* That one aged well—I'm still allergic to camping.

PART FIVE

SOCIAL MEDIA

When I choose which dances to put online, it's 100% *never* planned! It's very random—however I'm feeling that day is kind of the vibe. All the dances I post on TikTok are really fun and easy, for the most part. I know you can learn them too. ☺

BEHIND THE SCENES

TIPS FOR POSTING ON SOCIAL MEDIA:

* Be spontaneous! Be comfortable!
* Just post what you like—not simply to gain a following.
* Don't post anything that'll put other people down in the slightest.
* Keep some of yourself just for you—parts of your life should stay private.
* If you post what makes you happy, then you won't have to worry about keeping up an act.
* Clothes are for personal expression—wear what makes you comfortable.
* Post pictures you love even if they aren't "influencer" pictures. You don't have to be dolled up 24/7 to take a good photo.
* Post behind-the-scenes of your own life.
* Find a filter you love. Mine's a VSCO filter that I personalized.
* Respect people and, no matter what, be kind.
* Be yourself and have fun with it!

I have several favorite phone cases—a few of them are charging cases. I can never go without my phone being charged!

NEVER TRY TO BE SOMEONE YOU AREN'T. THIS APPLIES TO REAL LIFE AND ONLINE. PROJECTING A DIFFERENT ONLINE IDENTITY WOULD BE EASY, BUT I AM WHO I AM, AND THAT DOESN'T CHANGE—NO MATTER IF I'M CHATTING WITH DIXIE OR POSTING ONLINE!

TRUE TO MYSELF

There's only one person like you, and remember: You are enough!

CHARLI D'AMELIO

THE
TONIGHT
SHOW
JIMMY
FALLON

673S-9

Star Room

**EVERYTHING I DO
IS GENUINE—THAT'S
JUST WHO I AM.**

Like I said, for most of my photos, I use a VSCO filter that I customized. Here's the secret:

* AL3: all the way up
* Exposure: -1.7
* Contrast: -1.1
* Saturation up 0.3
* Skin tone down 0.9

PRO TIP!

Don't worry if you don't have fancy equipment to shoot your content. Half the time I'm grabbing the closest water bottle or paper towel roll to be my tripod for my phone. Just have fun and be in the moment and it will shine through in your content!

BE IN THE MOMENT

People think they know me, and then BOOM—I do something they weren't expecting. I like to keep people guessing.

I met my best friend at a dance class when I was twelve. We didn't go to the same school or anything, but when we met, it just clicked—and we've been BFFs ever since! You never know where you're going to meet someone who could end up as your best friend!

What's the weirdest way you have met a friend?

I HOPE PEOPLE SEE THAT I'M A REAL PERSON AND NOT JUST A GIRL THAT DANCES BEHIND YOUR PHONE SCREEN.

REAL TALK

I don't share a lot about myself online, and usually people ask me the same things about how I got to where I am now. I don't typically go into the backstory! My friends and I tend to live in the moment, too. So this book is my way of sharing more about myself with you!

ME!

My brand is so normal but like "My dog is my only friend"-type stuff: super, super weird. If you look at my Twitter, you'll probably never see me the same way!

GET CREATIVE

Usually when I post on TikTok, the type of content I create depends on whatever my mood or vibe is that day. Sometimes I challenge myself to see what I can do!

♪ **TikTok**
@charlidamelio

THERE'S NO ONE WAY TO BE CREATIVE. THERE ARE TONS OF WAYS! SOME PEOPLE LIKE TO PLAN THINGS OUT, AND SOME PEOPLE—LIKE ME—PREFER TO GO WITH WHAT THEY'RE FEELING. BE CREATIVE IN WHATEVER WAY FITS YOUR STYLE.

IF YOU'RE LOOKING TO GET CREATIVE:

* Listen to your energy—be attuned to yourself.
* Whenever you feel like making something, act on it.
* Embrace the challenge and put in the hard work!
* Just have fun and be nice! I was taught to be a friendly person. It really goes a long way.

LISTEN TO YOUR ENERGY

KEEP ON CREATING

EMBRACE CHALLENGES!

HAVE FUN!

CHARLI TRIVIA

I have a hard time picking my favorite color because I don't want any of the other colors to feel bad.

KEEP IT REAL

Who I am feels natural right now. Times change—I'll change, I'll grow up. But I'm happy right now, and any change—I hope— would be for the better.

My parents have their own social media accounts—they'll post old videos of our family, and I like having them there. TikTok is very entertaining—you're free to post whatever. My parents aren't embarrassing, but I keep an eye on their accounts just in case. ☺

COLLAB

I wanna collab with Emma Chamberlain or Madison Beer! Who would be your dream collab partners?

MAKE THINGS WITH FRIENDS

PART SIX

MAKING THE MOST OF ME TIME

Stuff I like best:

PAINTING

DANCE

NAILS

Making dance videos is really fun, but sometimes I just wanna hit pause! For self-care, it's all about the simple stuff like ice cream, a hot shower, or a cup of coffee. I also *love* getting my nails done, cuddling with my dogs, and using sheet masks. The simple stuff is all you really need!

What are your self-care routines?

SELF-CARE

My favorite movies and TV shows are:

THE GRINCH

THE CAT IN THE HAT

ORPHAN

YUM

If I could choose one meal for life, it would be chicken nuggets. From anywhere!

My rule of thumb: I need as much creative freedom as possible, or what I do isn't going to seem real.

On my Explore page on Instagram, I find people who make gourmet food or desserts. I *love* watching people bake. It's so crazy how talented some chefs are! I would really like to get to that level, but I'm not sure I could. I try to bake, but I seem to mess up even the simple stuff. I'm working on it!

My favorite treats are plain vanilla meringues or ice cream cake.

PART SEVEN

FAMILY

I'm not sure what type of family I want when I grow up. Kids, dogs, or both? It's like: Kids or dogs—which one is more work? I'm a lot of work, so if I have a child like me, that's just . . . well . . . ☺

SQUAD

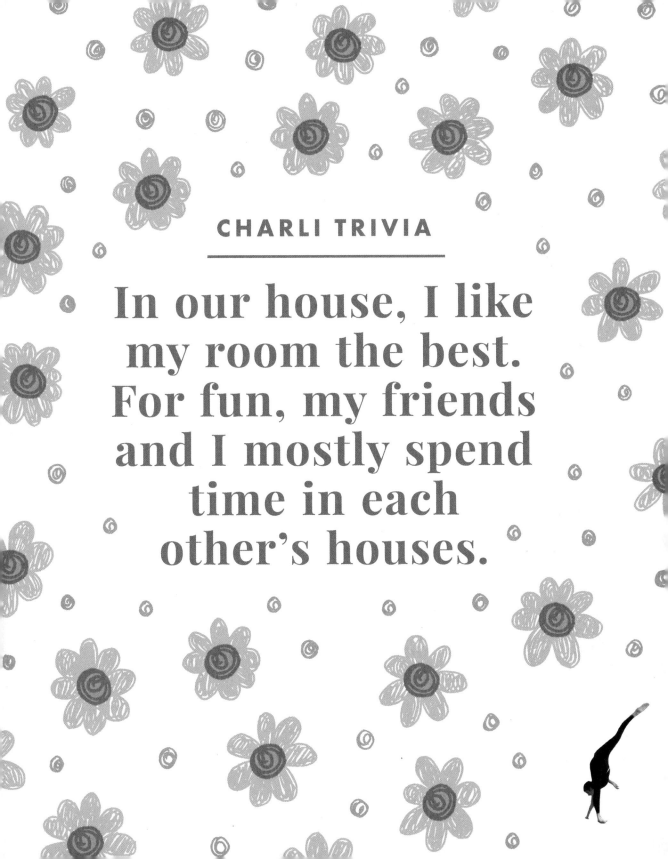

CHARLI TRIVIA

In our house, I like my room the best. For fun, my friends and I mostly spend time in each other's houses.

Most people wouldn't handle this crazy ride of mine as well as my family. It's pretty cool that I was given a family that is so ready for whatever is to come. My family has always been very close, and they'll back me up 100% if social media fails or if friends fail. I'm very grateful to have my family as a support system during all of this.

My family really likes ice cream,
and we love to watch movies together.
What brings your family together?
What do you enjoy doing together?

_____

_____

_____

_____

_____

_____

FAMILY TIME

My parents were never fans of telling me what to wear, because clothes are an expression of yourself and it's important to wear what makes you happy.

THE FAM

LOVE THEM

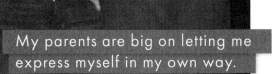

My parents are big on letting me express myself in my own way.

FAMILY

DIXIE AND I ARE VERY CLOSE—REALLY GOOD FRIENDS. WE'RE COMPLETELY DIFFERENT, BUT IT WORKS PERFECTLY:

* I'm quiet, and she's more outgoing.
* She's tall, and I'm shorter.
* She's sporty, and I'm the girly girl.
* We have very different senses of humor. Mine is sarcastic; I'm super dry, and you can never be sure whether it's a joke. Hers is very Millennial-style humor.

OUTGOING

QUIET

SHORT

SISTERS

TALL

SPORTY

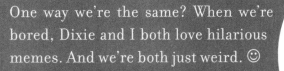
YouTube Space

GIRLY

MEME QUEEN

One way we're the same? When we're bored, Dixie and I both love hilarious memes. And we're both just weird. ☺

I call my grandmothers MaMa and Nett. MaMa lives in Connecticut, and Nett lives in Louisiana. I don't get to see Nett too often, but when I do, it's great. My grandmothers are the best, and they both make really good food. MaMa is super Italian, so her specialties are any kind of pasta, chicken cutlets, and mashed potatoes. And Nett makes Cajun food—mostly rice and gravy. Nett is on my mom's side, and MaMa is on my dad's side.

I'm close to both of my grandmothers.

FAMILY LOVE

What are some favorite foods your
family traditionally cooks?
What do they remind you of?

I'M A GOOD MIX OF MY PARENTS' TRAITS.

I turn to my mom for advice about emotional stuff. With my dad, I talk about problems he can help me work through. They both help me with issues, just different types. With my dad it's more like, "Oh, Dixie broke my computer, and I'm upset and angry and don't know what to do." And my dad will get it fixed. With my mom, it's more about friend stuff and breakups and things like that.

FAMILY FUN!

THE D'AMELIOS

Who do you turn to for advice, and when? What was a time that someone in your family came through for you when you were stuck?

FAM

I am grateful to have parents who are ready to support me no matter what I decide to do!

SUPPORT SYSTEM

PART EIGHT

RELATIONSHIPS

Relationships are beautiful, amazing, and sometimes hard, whether they're friendships, romantic partnerships, or family. I'm lucky to have a strong, supportive family in my parents, Dixie, my pups, and my extended family. And I've been fortunate to experience a million hilarious, fun times with friends and some sweet times with boyfriends.

But it hasn't always been easy! I've had a few fights with friends—luckily, we're pretty great at resolving conflict! In some cases, my friends and I have drifted apart over the years. (That's just a normal part of growing up.) My grandfather's death was super hard on me. And . . . let's just say not all romances are created equal. It would be really easy to let the hurtful times hold me back. But I know love is what makes life worthwhile, more than anything else. So I keep being brave and putting myself out there.

I'M SMART ABOUT WHO I GIVE MY HEART TO, AND I WILL NEVER BUILD WALLS AROUND IT.

Relationships—whether they end up being good or bad—allow you to learn a lot about yourself as a person. My previous experiences in relationships have taught me so much about myself in general, and I have grown into a stronger person because of how they went.

I'M HAPPIEST WHEN I SURROUND MYSELF WITH PEOPLE WHO MAKE ME FEEL 100% ACCEPTED JUST AS I AM.

Being in a relationship that is shown publicly on social media can be tricky at times, because if that relationship comes to an end, people feel like they have the right to know every little detail. Everyone deserves the time and space to process the ups and downs of a relationship in private, though. So that is what I've tried to do in the past, and it's definitely helped me heal and grow stronger.

RELATIONSHIPS ARE BASED ON TRUST AND HONESTY.

I trust my sister, Dixie, completely. We tell each other everything, and because she's older, she usually gives me good advice.

Owning your mistakes is one of the best ways to build healthy relationships.

IF YOU CONFRONT ME HONESTLY ABOUT SOMETHING I DID TO HURT YOU—EVEN IF I DIDN'T MEAN TO—I WILL ALWAYS LISTEN TO YOU AND RESPECT YOU. A TRUE FRIEND CARES HOW THEY MAKE OTHER PEOPLE FEEL.

The thing I hate most in the world is lying. If I know that someone is lying to me, that's the worst feeling ever. And because I know it's so hurtful, I try my best never to lie. Even if I slip up and do lie, I feel an obligation to own up to it. First of all, I feel bad—I have the worst guilty conscience ever and don't like the idea of hurting people. And second of all, the truth almost always comes out—it's pointless not to own your mistakes!

ADVICE FOR A BROKEN HEART:

* The idea of restarting is often harder than the actual restart. Be brave, and you'll feel 100% better in the end.

* Remind yourself that if you find out that someone isn't your person, what's the point of keeping that going?

* If someone isn't treating you right, and you know in your heart you deserve better in the way they treat you and make you feel, it's not worth it.

* The longer you stay in it, the harder it is to get away.

BE BRAVE

My favorite ice cream flavors are vanilla and chocolate chip cookie dough.

If you are in a relationship that doesn't bring you joy—friendship, romantic, whatever—work up the courage to leave as soon as you can. If someone isn't making you feel good about yourself, it's important to get away. Not only will it do more damage the longer you stick around, but you'll also feel really empowered and confident when you're brave enough to walk away. If you feel like it's too hard, just repeat this mantra: *Be braver than you've ever been.* You can do it! I have, and now I'm happier than ever.

And at the beginning of that friendship or relationship—listen to your gut. Sometimes I'll be talking to a new friend and the vibes are just off. And then I'm just like . . . *No, this person doesn't have my best interests at heart.* It took a little practice, but now I know to listen hard to my inner voice and always trust what it's telling me. It takes a lot of courage to walk away from something that isn't good for you!

TOXIC

NO BAD VIBES

REAL TALK

I don't have celebrity crushes—I've never been a fangirl.

YOU'RE LOVED

For me, leaving toxic relationships behind and turning to my family and trusted friends for support has always kicked off the healing process. Remember: You are loved.

What has made you feel better after you've had a relationship with a friend or partner fall apart? How did you build yourself back up?

_____

_____

_____

_____

_____

_____

_____

SEEING MY PARENTS HAVE A HAPPY, SUPPORTIVE RELATIONSHIP HAS SET AN IMPORTANT EXAMPLE FOR WHAT I WANT IN A RELATIONSHIP.

MOM AND DAD

ROLE MODELS

My parents were married in their midtwenties. They met in New York City. My mom moved from Louisiana to New York, and my dad already lived in New York. My mom was a personal trainer at a gym, and my dad's friend met her and brought the two of them together. They're the cutest.

PART NINE

IN THE PUBLIC EYE

I LOVE MY LIFE, BUT EVERY NOW AND THEN I WANT TO HIT PAUSE.

Then I realize how much my life has changed for the better. I dance and post to have fun—and I'm still having fun. Although sometimes unkind comments can be hurtful, I see them as opportunities to exercise strength.

There are so many amazing things that have come from this journey; but even without my online following, I'd still be making videos dancing. I'd be doing the exact same thing I'm doing now! It isn't about getting attention; it's about doing what I love.

And just like anyone else, when I get tired of being onscreen, I can take some time alone to recharge.

DO WHAT YOU LOVE

HAVE FUN

LISTEN TO YOURSELF
AND BE AWARE OF
WHAT YOU NEED AT
ANY GIVEN MOMENT.

DISCONNECT

CHILL

When you do most feel the need to disconnect?

_____

_____

_____

_____

_____

_____

_____

_____

BRB

The question I'm asked the most is "How did all this happen?" I would tell you if I knew, but the thing is, I actually have no idea!

I'm very, very shy. When people meet me, they're always like, "Wow, you're more shy than I thought you were going to be!" But once I warm up to people, I'm very outgoing.

MEETING J.LO AT THE SUPER BOWL WAS CRAZY.

Nothing seemed real—it was like one big dream, like I was gonna wake up and everything would go back to normal.

When I met J.Lo, I couldn't even think straight. I couldn't even think at all! She was like, "Hey, I hope you liked the dance we did." She said her daughters watch me online. J.Lo's dancing was crazy—she's so good! She was super normal when I met her and really, really sweet and genuine about everything. It was very nice to see.

I would love to act one day. I started with voice-over acting for *Stardog and Turbocat*. I enjoyed that and would love to do it again.

It's hard to know what my next big dreams will be, because dancing with J.Lo was one I had for so long, and I wasn't expecting it to happen so soon! I'm not sure what comes next, but I'll think of something.

What are the biggest dreams you'd like to achieve? Who of anyone in the world would you most want to hang out with?

_____

_____

_____

_____

_____

_____

_____

When I was on *The Tonight Show Starring Jimmy Fallon*, I wasn't super nervous, but I was once again like, "Who let me come here?!" Jimmy was super, super sweet, and we got along great. Appearing on the show was a very easygoing process, and everyone I interacted with was genuine and fun to be around. I feel like that's the best way to choose who you collaborate with—it should always feel natural and easy.

BACKSTAGE!

My *Live with Kelly and Ryan* interview was the first time in history where there was no live audience, and my appearance on *The Tonight Show Starring Jimmy Fallon* was the last time the show had a live audience before the coronavirus pandemic. It was a crazy experience.

I love this Miu Miu dress that I wore on the show! I felt so confident in it.

When I became the first person to cross 50 million followers on TikTok, it was weird, very weird. I was sleeping when it happened!

iHeartRadio's 2019 Jingle Ball was my very first red-carpet experience! It was at Madison Square Garden in NYC, and I got to see some of my favorite artists: Lizzo, Taylor Swift, Halsey, and a bunch of others. Dixie and I both wore black—I paired my jeans with a glittery black-and-silver top, and Dixie wore a snakeskin bralette with high-waisted leather pants. The whole thing was hectic and amazing.

SO FUN!

I can sing
my ABCs backward.

Q: What part of being on social media is really hard?

A: The comments and hate I sometimes receive. One of the most frustrating comments I get is "Why do you have the hype?" It's like, I have no idea why I have the hype. This isn't something I chose—it just sort of happened. I'm trying to handle it the best way I can and focus on the positives.

PART TEN

GIVING BACK

A QUICK WORD ON BULLYING:

When this all started, I would be very quick to defend myself. Then I realized there are many people who make comments and videos about me, and I can't respond to all of them or change anyone's minds if they're looking for a reason to disike me.

A lot of people say things about me that aren't true. It's hard not to give in to the negativity at times; it hurts so much. I still don't know the best way to deal with it, but one tip I'd give: Don't check comments so much—in fact, try to look as little as possible. My mom and dad say, "We don't know these negative people, and it's not worth giving them your time and energy."

SPREAD POSITIVITY

I think my favorite thing is to hear people say I got them back into dancing, or I've helped them in some other way. Knowing that what I do is helping people makes all of the bad stuff seem unimportant.

Dixie and I partnered with UNICEF on an anti-bullying campaign. We wanted to make sure to convey important messages: that people need to be nice, and bullying is hurtful and not OK.

BULLYING IS FRIGHTENINGLY COMMON ON THE INTERNET.

Even before I was online, people were not nice. You have to find your people, and I want to help others do that.

FIND YOUR PEOPLE

I have made mistakes along my journey—everyone has. I have learned and grown from those experiences, and my personal growth has inspired me to give back however I can. It feels so good to be able to help people in some small way, even if it's just with a smile or kind words. There are so many things I want to do! I am taking it one step at a time and hope to do as much as I can to make a difference in the world.

I'M PASSIONATE ABOUT:

ANTI-BULLYING

ANIMAL RIGHTS

MAKING A DIFFERENCE

What causes are you most passionate about? How can you help make a difference in your neighborhood or on a larger scale?

MAKING A DIFFERENCE

IF I COULD SOLVE ONE GLOBAL PROBLEM, IT WOULD BE SAFETY. I WANT EVERYONE TO FEEL SAFE, NO MATTER WHERE THEY ARE OR WHAT THEY'RE DOING.

REAL TALK

I choose projects based on whether they have positive messages and if they align with my values. If it's a good thing, I want to share it with the world.

If I could be granted one wish, it would be that the kind people of the world would all rise to the top and spread their kindness widely. I believe in karma 100%.

IT'S GREAT THAT I HAVE BEEN GIVEN A PLATFORM TO BE A ROLE MODEL!

YOU'RE WORTH IT

I love sharing the things that are important to me with my followers. I especially hope to make people who are feeling rejected or insecure know that they are loved and appreciated for who they are.

I'M TRYING TO SHOW PEOPLE THAT NO MATTER WHO YOU ARE, YOU'RE WORTH IT.

Be the best version of yourself you can be, and everything will be OK.

KIND

POSITIVE

A GOOD ROLE MODEL IS SOMEONE WHO IS BRAVE ENOUGH TO SPEAK THE TRUTH AND ALWAYS READY TO LIFT PEOPLE UP.

BRAVE

GRACIOUS

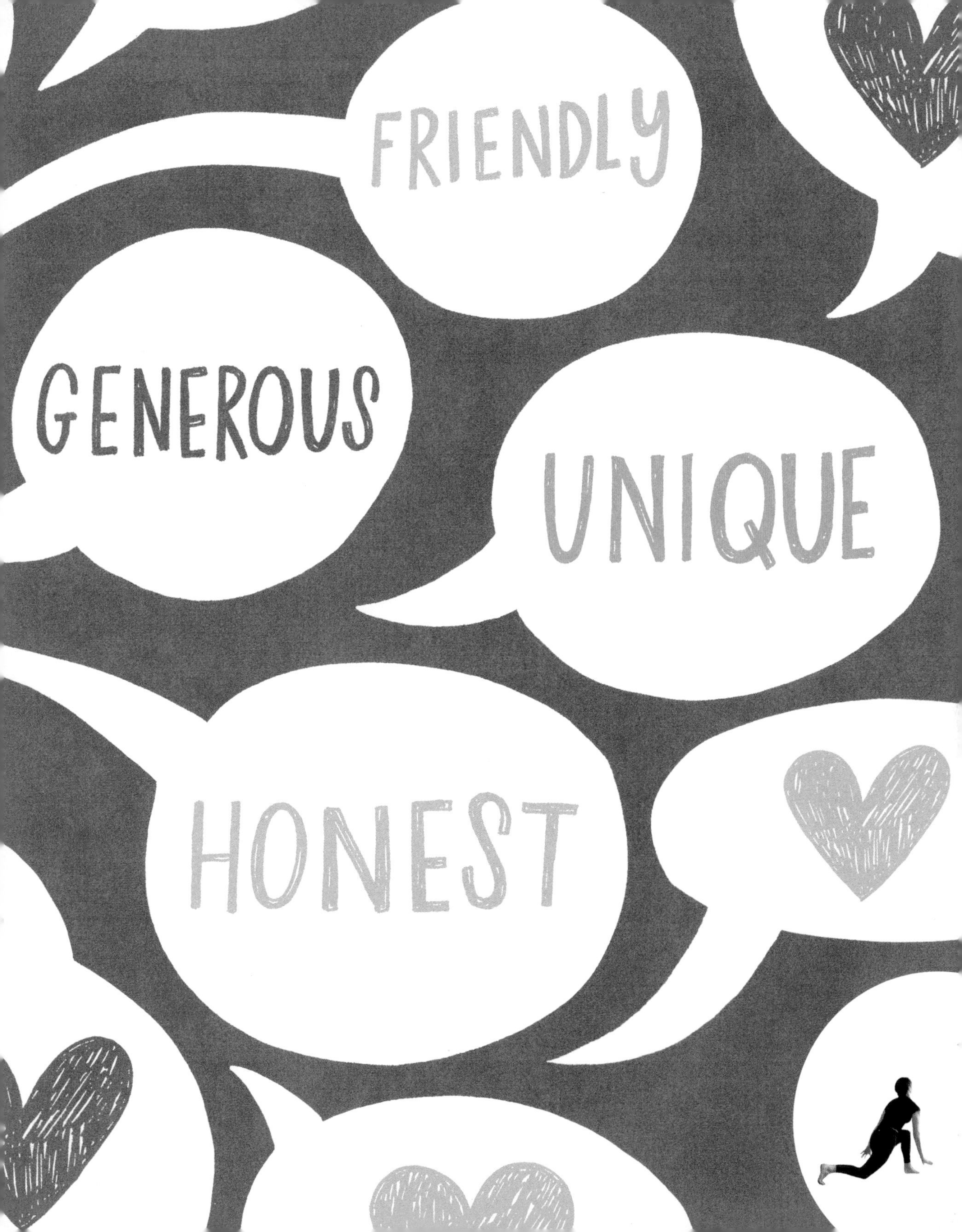
FRIENDLY
GENEROUS
UNIQUE
HONEST

ACKNOWLEDGMENTS

To my mom and dad; my sister, Dixie; and my friends: Thanks for always being there for me whenever I need you. I can't imagine going through this crazy life without you.

Team Charli: Thanks to everyone on my team who supports me and who has helped me realize dreams I never even knew I had.

Special thanks to Brandi Bowles at United Talent Agency and Anne Heltzel, Amy Vreeland, and Jessica Gotz from Abrams Books for guiding me through the process of creating my first book (and for letting me have stickers!).

Thank you to Steph Stilwell for illustrating and designing and Brenda Angelilli for art directing this amazing book that really captures my style.

Thank you to all of the awesome photographers who provided pictures for this book: Zusha Goldin (40, 49), Jordan Matter (60), Lance Sanchez (70, 84), Jake Doolittle (73, 75), Daniel Diamond (98, 116, 125, 128, 131, 140), and Bryant Eslava (110).